EYE TO EYE WITH DOGS

SHIH TZU

Lynn M. Stone

Rourke
Publishing LLC
Vero Beach, Florida 32964

www.rourkepublishing.com

PHOTO CREDITS: All photos © Lynn M. Stone

Editor: Meg Greve

Cover and page design by Nicola Stratford

Library of Congress Cataloging-in-Publication Data

Stone, Lynn M.
  Shih tzu / Lynn M. Stone.
     p. cm. -- (Eye to eye with dogs)
  Includes index.
  ISBN 978-1-60472-366-3
  1. Shih tzu--Juvenile literature. I. Title.
  SF429.S64S76 2009
  636.76--dc22
                                        2008012980

Printed in the USA

CG/CG

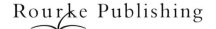

Rourke Publishing

www.rourkepublishing.com – rourke@rourkepublishing.com
Post Office Box 3328, Vero Beach, FL 32964

Table of Contents

The Shih Tzu   5

Looks   8

Shih Tzus of the Past   12

The Dog for You?   17

A Note about Dogs   22

Glossary   23

Index   24

The American Kennel Club groups the shih tzu with the toy breeds because of its small size.

The Shih Tzu

The shih tzu has its roots in ancient Asia. The Chinese called the shih tzu *lion dog* or *little lion*. They thought these furry little dogs looked much like their carved figures of lions. Sometimes the spunky little shih tzu acts like it is the king of beasts!

SHIH TZU FACTS

Weight: 9 to 16 pounds
   (4 to 7 kilograms)
Height: 9 to 11 inches
   (23 to 28 centimeters)
Country of Origin:
   China
Life Span: 12 to 14 years

The shih tzu's long hair has much to do with its likeness to a miniature lion. A male African lion has a long **mane** that grows only around its face. However, long hair covers the shih tzu's whole body.

The owner of this 13-year-old shih tzu braided her hair.

This armful of shih tzus weighs about 20 pounds (9 kilograms).

The shih tzu is one of the toy dog **breeds**. It is a true lap dog. It weighs between nine to sixteen pounds (4 to 7 kilograms). A newborn lion cub weighs about four pounds (2 kilograms) at birth and soon weighs more than the little lion dog.

The shih tzu is a gentle, lively pooch with an outgoing personality. It is friendly and trusting, too.

Looks

A fully furred shih tzu has a long, flowing coat. A second, shorter coat lies under the long outer fur. The coat hides the dog's short legs and solid body.

A clipped shih tzu shows the dog's short legs.

This shih tzu can see better because of its topknot.

A shih tzu's fur can be almost any color. It can be a solid color or a mix of colors. Owners tie the long fur atop a shih tzu's head into a topknot. Beneath the eyes, the long fur sweeps into a moustache.

The shih tzu's dark eyes are large, round, and spread apart. The breed has a square **muzzle** and wide nostrils. The shih tzu's tail arches over its back, like a fountain of fur.

A shih tzu shows off its curled tail.

Shih Tzus of the Past

The exact **ancestry** of the shih tzu is not clear. It is clear, however, that the shih tzu is an old breed. Asian art of 1,400 years ago shows small dogs that resemble the modern shih tzu.

People in Tibet probably developed one or more of the shih tzu's ancestors. Today Tibet is part of China.

The shih tzu looks much like its ancestors from Tibet.

The shih tzu's large eyes are similar to those of the Pekinese.

The shih tzu most likely resulted from **crosses** between small Tibetan dogs and ancestors of China's Pekinese dogs. The Chinese probably brought the little Tibetan dogs to China in the 1600s.

Maintenance bands help keep a young shih tzu's facial hair in place.

Chinese royalty kept shih tzus. They earned another nickname, *chrysanthemum-faced dogs*. The chrysanthemum blossom is round, something like the shih tzu's head. In addition, the chrysanthemum has thick petals, just as a shih tzu has thick facial hair.

China was a stage for warfare during many of the first 50 years of the last century. Warfare meant hard times for the shih tzu. The breed nearly became **extinct**.

Once nearly extinct, the shih tzu has become one of the most popular dog breeds in the United States.

A Chinese fortune cookie would have predicted an uncertain future for the shih tzu. However, the breed had good fortune after all. An Englishman took a few shih tzus back home. The English liked the shih tzu and began **breeding** them in 1930.

American soldiers brought shih tzus to the United States from Europe after World War II (1939-1945). By the 1960s, China's lion dogs had become popular in American homes.

The Dog for You?

The shih tzu is an indoor dog. However, like most other small indoor dog breeds, a shih tzu likes to play and needs exercise. It enjoys a walk on a leash and active indoor games.

A short hike provides a shih tzu with sunshine and exercise.

Shih tzu owners often describe their dogs as sweet. That is because a shih tzu is highly affectionate. It will likely be friendly to strangers and patient with small children.

Shih tzus seem to be as fond of people as people are of them!

Shih tzus are too small and friendly to be guard dogs, but their barks make them good watchdogs.

At the same time, a shih tzu may startle easily and bark. A little shih tzu cannot guard the house. It is not the ideal guard dog. However, it does make a good watchdog.

Shih tzus in dog shows wear their furry coats long and carefully groomed. Owners must brush their coats at least every other day.

Daily brushing keeps a shih tzu's coat free from tangles and matting.

Shih tzus do not do well in hot climates, so this shih tzu living in Florida is clipped for comfort.

A long coat can be very warm for this little dog. In the warm months, many shih tzu owners clip their dogs' long coats. Less hair helps them stay cool.

A Note about Dogs

Puppies are cute and cuddly, but only after serious thought should anybody buy one. Puppies, after all, grow up.

A dog will require more than love and patience. It will need healthy food, exercise, grooming, medical care, and a warm, safe place to live.

A dog can be your best friend, but you need to be its best friend, too.

Choosing the right breed for you requires homework. For more information about buying and owning a dog, contact the American Kennel Club or the Canadian Kennel Club.

Glossary

ancestry (AN-sess-tree): the animals that at some past time were part of the modern animal's family

breeds (BREEDS): particular kinds of domestic animals within larger, closely related groups, such as the shih tzu

breeding (BREED-ing): the choosing of dog parents to produce pups

crosses (KRAWSS-ez): animals that are born of parents of different breeds

extinct (ek-STINGKT): to no longer exist

mane (MAYN): the hair of the head and neck, especially of a male lion

muzzle (MUHZ-uhl): the nose and jaw section of a dog's head

Index

Asia   5

breeds   7, 17

China   5, 13, 15, 16

chrysanthemum   14

coat   8, 20, 21

Europe   16

lion   5, 6, 7

Pekinese dogs   13

Tibet   12

topknot   10

toy dog   7

watchdog   19

Further Reading

American Kennel Club. *The Complete Dog Book*. American Kennel Club, 2006.

Gagne, Tammy. *Shih Tzu*. TFH Publications, 2006.

White, Joann. *Shih Tzu: Your Happy, Healthy Pet*. John Wiley & Sons, 2005.

Website to Visit

http://www.akc.org/breeds/shih_tzu/index.cfm
http://www.shihtzu.org
www.ckc.ca/

About the Author

Lynn M. Stone is a widely-published wildlife and domestic animal photographer and the author of more than 500 children's books. His book *Box Turtles* was chosen as an Outstanding Science Trade Book and Selectors' Choice for 2008 by the Science Committee of the National Science Teachers' Association and the Children's Book Council.

DATE DUE

MR 26			
AP 21 '09			
AP 29 '09			
JE 25 '09			
OC 28 '09			
FE 25 '10			
OC 26 '10			
NO 09 '1			
AP 04 '1			
AG 22 '1			
JA 31 '12			
MR 07 '12			
JY 11 '12			
DE 27 '12			
JY 16 '13			
JY 23 '14			
JE 11 '15			
GAYLORD			PRINTED IN U.S.A.